The Champion of Doubt

poems by

Tom Driscoll

Finishing Line Press
Georgetown, Kentucky

The Champion of Doubt

Copyright © 2023 by Tom Driscoll
ISBN 979-8-88838-206-6 First Edition
All rights reserved under International and Pan-American Copyright Conventions.
No part of this book may be reproduced in any manner whatsoever without written permission from the publisher, except in the case of brief quotations embodied in critical articles and reviews.

Publisher: Leah Huete de Maines
Editor: Christen Kincaid
Cover Art and Design: Denise Driscoll—acrylic painting on wood panel 'Triangles 4' (denisedriscoll.com).
Author Photo: Dan Tappan

Order online: www.finishinglinepress.com
also available on amazon.com

Author inquiries and mail orders:
Finishing Line Press
P. O. Box 1626
Georgetown, Kentucky 40324
U. S. A.

Table of Contents

I

Birches 1

"John" 2

What to say on loneliness 3

Check-out time 4

No such thing 5

Mary and John 6

Quincy Street 7

On Point 8

Gettysburg, 1963 9

To History 10

Yellow Photograph 12

The Clarity of Water 13

Hold your tongue 16

The Rakes 17

II

The king has been a prisoner 21

#4 Cook Street 22

Cinéma vérité 23

Rural free delivery 24

Off the boat 25

The future that used to be 27

One Who Climbs Mountains 28

The water tower 29

Chapter 7 30

Always Sunday 31

The old soldier's cats..32

Elegy 34

The Other Guitar 35

This isn't the first time I tried..36

III

Border Music..41

Shelter Cove 42

That summer of monuments..43

Always July 44

Stone Mountain, Georgia 45

Quaking Aspen 47

D&C 48

At General Sherman's keep...49

If you see the Buddha..50

Like a glove...52

Keepsake shirt...54

Pharoah's Horsemen..55

The Whistlepig...56

Then and there...57

IV

Notes on demolition...61

The box spring 64

The recording session..65

Cynthia's time..66

Always love..67

Guitars..68

Memorial familiar 69

The way it is...70

Empathy...71

Citizen Cain 72

The Widow's House..73

The Champion of Doubt..74

Joy...75

That River 76

*"...for the one who doubts is like a wave
of the sea that is driven and tossed by the wind."*

~ James 1:6

I

Birches

Three birches, one stands apart
leans away, seeming about to fall
—this at the edge of a narrow stand
of woods, oak mostly;

the birches' black markings
at this distance in the misty light
distracted sketches of some dreaming artist;
papery bark peeling in places—
the pencil shavings.

My father once told me how birches were known
as "sentries of the forest" as they had this habit
of appearing at the edge of a deeper woods,
spare, pale, as if keeping watch.
They were a frail species, he said, their health
bespoke that of the forest they supposedly guarded.
It was something of the soil, their tendency towards light.

Delicate witnesses, they'd fail first as a warning.

"John"

In that house it was rare to call someone
by their given name. We were all about
the banter—
aliases and insults—
I wouldn't call them pet names.

So, I knew there was trouble
in the way she simply said my name; so calm, plain.

My own response was the usual aggravation.
Whaaat?—I yelled and, without an answer, I settled deeper
in my chair in the den watching whatever it was on the television.

Then it began to work on me, just the sound
of her saying my name, none of the usual salt and spit.
In all our years, you know, I never laid a hand on her.
I can, at least, say that much.

But that night I let her have it—wham—across the chops
—everything I had.
I'd found her fallen in a heap at the top of the stairs.
Blue, not breathing.
Man, I really belted her, hit her twice.

She gasped a breath then, that second time. What a sound
her breath. From there we made it to the hospital, somehow in time.
I don't remember much about how we got there.
What I remember is striking her.

And the strange sense that had come of hearing her simply say my name.

What to say on loneliness

When I worked at Frank's Mobil it was a full-service station.
Now you'd be lucky to find where they sell
the windshield washer fluid. You pump the gas yourself,
purchase snacks at a convenience store.
Out back, where there used to be nothing but woods
and a couple of narrow logging paths, there is now
what you'd call a *suburban shopping plaza*
anchored by a regional grocery store chain,
a couple of nationally advertised restaurant franchises,
clothing retailers. The bank from uptown built
a new building there, I think on account
of the parking. There is a sea of parking.

I learned to run the lifts in the service bays at Frank's;
did oil changes when the pumps were slow, changed
a muffler or two. I could drive the wrecker and do road calls,
practically ran the station alone several nights a week
and the occasional weekend Frank wanted to give himself a break.
495 wasn't yet completed then, the last few miles down toward
the Cape were still in construction. There was no one on that road
late at night. After work I'd drive my old blue Ford XL-LTD convertible
just to see how fast I could
get it going before it started to shake
—the alignment never right after my brother's crack up
from back when he had the use of the car.

I'd just drive with my music blaring,
sometimes, just the sound of the engine was enough.

I'd just drive, drive to the end; to this pool of yellow light after miles of darkness
where all the heavy road construction vehicles waited on the next day's work.

Check-out time

The work crew has built an ad hoc scaffold
of wracking aluminum ladders and plank

all roped together to stage the north side gable
where the rustic clapboard's gone punky soft.

Years of harsh weather and not enough light.
Tall pines shadow that side of the house

such that it never dries after a storm. Wrong paint
retains the moisture too, rots the pine board—

it crumbles at the touch. And we've come to learn, at some pain,
the damaged wood serves nicely as a nesting place for wasps.

My father hired a contractor to tear it all out,
hang aluminum siding—so unlike him

not to assign the task to one of his sons. Each of us painted
that side of the house at least once, tried stop-gap repairs.

Now I smell the sickly-sweet poison as it sprays from a store-bought can.
"It's check out time, guys"—I hear the crew boss say this

first under his breath, a note-to-self not the wasps, as he's leaned out
from his swaying perch high on the scaffold to inspect, search

ravaged nests for last angry survivors. He tips the spray can
back and forth in one hand, listening at the metallic tic of the pea inside.

His eyes squinting almost closed into a gunslinger's leer,
"It's check out time," he repeats, this time as an aside

performed in stage whisper for the audience
below that he pretends not to notice.

No such thing

The old house gutted, plaster board
torn away to pull antiquated wiring
for new plumbing and heating upgrade planned,
a modern, more real estate marketable kitchen.

Hardwood floors might have been reclaimed
but for the places the damage ran deep. The roof leaked,
pipes leaked, too. Too long there were too many cats.
And I am sorry to see the small windows each side

of the fireplace lost, framed in and sided over.
They were favorites of his, the way they caught
the light at certain hours. We used to agree on that
—how there really was no such thing as too much light.

Mary and John

Shadow of a smile one side of her mouth,
she'd address him by his last name—'Driscoll'—
with the wry coloring of irony in her tone as she did,
as if to admit, once married, forever that way
despite divorce, still they were not
so close as to be on a first name basis—'Driscoll'—

Across that old kitchen table, with the folding leaf
each side—and the one that always sagged—
he'd have made coffee—terrible coffee
but somehow his tea was worse.
She'd sit as his guest in the house she had let him
have, she reminded him.
They shared a laugh
at that, at the quality of her legal representation.
Her superannuated attorney arrived in court, his shuffling
feet in carpet slippers, papers stuffed into an accordion folder.
'A regular Clarence Darrow, that one,' he laughed, just a little
too hard. She nodded, offered that staged sigh of hers, then hint at a smile.

She'd taken 'Driscoll' to his doctor that day. He no longer drove.
I met them both there in that kitchen
                                        that day.

Come to think of it, you never heard him say her name either.
There was the mock formality he'd use as one approach.
He would address her as 'Ma'am'—Yes, ma'am,' he'd answer her
and it would irk her just about as much as he intended.
'Gladys' was another form of address, an alias, harsh,
slapstick, some invented character borrowed from another comedy.

Speaking of her, to me or to one of my brothers, he would refer to her
as 'The War Department' to consign institutional status
to what he accused in her, what he pitied in her, what he loved
so grudgingly, her fears, her frightful tenacious authority.

I don't believe I ever heard him simply say her name.

Quincy Street

That house on Quincy Street
he bought them with GI Bill money
he should've used to buy his own—our own
—they'd just moved into the place.
We were there for a visit with her
that day, the day she died—
that day his mother died.

I know how he told you many times
about her last words and all.
"My mother's come to take me home."
Whenever he told you that story
I always remembered the part
he did not tell; how he left the house then,
walked out into the yard
and stood there alone.
I tried to be there with him—
to reach him somehow.
But he was alone, so insistingly alone.
I watched him from what I thought
was a safe distance thereafter.
I was pregnant with your brother
and had gone back inside the house.
I knew I could not comfort him,
could only watch what burned there
that would never stop its burning.
He stood, his back turned to the house, to me,
to everyone—everything—his own sadness.

The grass wasn't yet growing in the soil
they'd graded in the yard.
I remember how it began to rain, how
from each of the first raindrops
that fell around him dust rose
in small puffs of smoke.

On Point

Posed, two porcelain hounds,
one with his tail broken off,
smears of dirt-mottled glue—
the different attempts at repair.

His once beautiful, gloss red-brown enamel
coat is masked in a yellowed greasiness,
odd product of dust and the years
of flawed effort to clean it away,

testimony to a particularly inept domesticity.
The dogs point atop a mock mahogany plinth
in stride and seeming about to spring
at the trail of their marked prey.

As historian, I can solemnly attest
the fugitive was never found.

Gettysburg, 1963

I'd been told we'd be climbing a tower
and pictured something more solidly made

of stone, not this gray metal scaffold
that seems to weigh each of us as we climb

with some tensing in the cross-brace cables
registering our steps on the open stair, tread by tread,

rungs on a twisted ladder. My hand on the cool pipe rail,
wet with dew, I am just awake and sense I could easily fall.

This is to be our long last look out across the battlefield.
Early morning. Mist rising out of the long grass.

This structure placed in among a thinning stand of black pine
at the edge of the more exposed open field.

Not a trace of wind and my brothers and my father
are quiet as well. My mother waits down below in the car.

I'm a ghost climbed up here into the clouds, cool smoke
mixing with something once important and forgotten.

Today we'll have an early start at the driving,
'll be on the interstate by the time this has cleared.

To History

I suppose all those who seek you bring their biases,
bad habits of claiming to speak on your behalf.
And I'm no better—

I've my own theories
about your narrative arc spanning
different generations—

how my father carried that jug of tears
from his own father's life;
both men abandoned to grief and guilt as children,

left with that scald and scar of remaining—
one mother dead, the other diseased,
fathers of each blind with blaming.

Hard luck stories... Dad would tell me
there was more to you than that,
and he would tell me I had a fine, steady hand

as I poured whiskey and approached
another of our stupid debates on your account—

Man's inhumanity to man...
the extraordinary accomplishments of one generation
as opposed to another...

Drink transmogrified pain to silly sickness, cloying
sweet and unsteady talk of nations and ideals,
wet ash on grey stone, chipped glass,

sentimental music, vague and sour
bombast, nausea—arguing abstractions
we neither of us grasped   quite.

And you, History, you were the Queen of Ultimate Questions
—you were the Kept Bitch of men claiming victory—

—you were a Logical Being—cruel—absurd—insistent
—senseless.

Our arguments borne out in repetition under the witness
of his two disdaining cats, the gorgeous light of a low sun,
late and glowing. That room, the scent of smoke
—both of us burning.

Yellow Photograph

I'm almost certain it's of my mother in her younger days—
the woman's affected the pose of a pinup girl or Hollywood starlet
the way they were in movie magazines

back in that day—the era of McCarthy hearings,
American-made black-and-white television sets, the bomb.

She's looked off into the distance, stage right,
posed in a clearing next to a pond.

Light behind her, features softened, even blurred, edges
confused in among those of the shadowing leaves; lower brush
and the branches hung down from above together occluding daylight.

This must have been my father's camera work.
I believe I recognize the scene as his cousin's camp

by Curlew Pond, he had the borrow of the place
whenever he wanted it, back then.

Dad could diagram for you how a camera lens worked
and never could take a decent picture.

He must have asked her to fold her legs beneath her, turn her face
in profile in just this way, place one hand on the ground at her side
just slightly behind her.

The other hand rests in her lap, her empty palm facing up.
Yes, he must have posed her this way. Her face, her eyes obscured,
yellowish light tracing the line of her cheek
—the one thing telling it's her.

The Clarity of Water

after Gregory Orr

for my uncle, John Carey

To dream of them without trouble
would be to not dream of them at all.

1 BORN OUT OF WATER

The body is smooth, slender, luminous,
perfect—so pale bright. It could be carved
from marble, so still as it lay there.
The man's head is turned to one side.

The boy is shaken by this vision,
its searing light, his sudden place
as witness to what he knows
no one wants him to see.

In years to come he will recall
the moment so many times
he'll start to believe this was the day
he arrived within his own body, crawled
up inside to watch the world through its eyes.

2

Two young boys and their uncle
swim by a floating dock.
The uncle believes he guards the young swimmers
and the boys tell themselves *they* are watching *him*.
First three voices ring off the pond's shimmering surface
—patina green, flashes of white.

Then the one boy's panicked scream
calling the uncle's name three times, then silence,
then he calls it out once more, differently.

3

I stand in the shallow water by the pond edge.
Small translucent fishes dart in around
my feet. Within their shadows, cast
on the gravelly bottom, are other shadows.

These are like fish dreams of other fishes
no one sees but me.

4 THE WATER

"Out beyond the dock
Pond weed was grown in thick
at the edge of deeper water.
Thank god he was as pale as he was,
his Irish skin, years of working nights,
sleeping most days—he was white
and bright as a bone
just settling into the dark bottom
as I found him that last time I dived.
I doubt I could have gone one more.
And your mother, she was no swimmer.
I remember she'd walked out as far as she could,
the water up to her chin she stretched out her hand.
It was the last I had left when our fingertips touched.
Christ, his body was cold. I had him under one arm."

5

There is another version of this life
where he was not injured as a child, his damaged brain
is whole, he is not subject to the seizures
that always came, as if to torture him, worst when he
tried again and again to learn to read.
His face isn't scarred.

He tells me that I should come meet his son,
that we would be—*thick as thieves.*

6 BREATH

There are nights I pray for you even though
I haven't your faith—I know there are worse things
than being mistaken. Clear water spills from your mouth
as they turn your face to one side and work
your, for the moment, lifeless body.
My father presses his mouth to yours.
Then that first breath,
your stone body's slightest answer.

7. THE COLOR OF LIGHT

The summer I was seven years old, Norman's camp
on Curlew Pond, it was time I should learn to swim.
I'd been told never go in less than twenty minutes
after eating.   The pond was deep, fed by cold springs
and it frightened me.
And so
I ate almost all the time, watched my brothers swim
from a distance, the shaded cabin ashore.

Fifty years and I still remember the sight of his scarred and swollen nose
disfigured, dark purple—side effect of the medication
he'd had to take his whole life.
We'd all learned to look away and not remind him.
That day in a pool of panic and sunlight it was the only color for miles.

Hold your tongue

The silence 'd suit him better—
better than anything you might
think to say:

complaint—the dry scrape
of noise and nuisance—pointless.

Didn't he teach you that
in the long run, that silence
could be as cutting?

Let others announce pride and rage
and sing
—what he had seen
and we never quite learned, what
marked him, seared and scarred him

closed his lips
with its burning kiss.

Hold your tongue and mind the fire.

The Rakes

Words are about as useless as memories
after all—ah, but remember

—you small enough I could pick you up
off the floor, how I'd start out humming
'The Rakes of Mallow'—that was the signal.
You knew it was time and folded yourself
into shape for the carrying.
I'd take you up, up the narrow wooden stair
to your bed—beery breath and beard stubble
the sharp caress to bless your sleep.

"Goodnight, sweet prince, may flights of angels
guide thee to thy rest."
I said that each time, as much to myself as you,
something between a joke and a prayer.
As I think of it now, it's that other Shakespearean
line that's telling—that one where "—the rest is silence."

It's about that silence, son,
what's taken you these years to forgive.
We both know it's not there weren't things
left to say; just that words would not say them.

For all the love of language, there was nothing fit
to ask your blessing.
I only stood from that last good kitchen chair,
even as you told me to sit, sit—you were leaving
but would come again tomorrow
tomorrow.

I crossed the room and I took your hand.
It didn't matter then that you did not understand
and I don't know that it matters now
—whether or not.
There is still nothing but time
and no man ever need say more than his prayers.

II

The king has been a prisoner

What I do recall is that I'd driven all night, the car
I'd borrowed, that it was still dark as I arrived.

Michael on the porch, perhaps he smoked
that long-stemmed clay pipe of his, the house
dark, the others asleep
—or had they moved away by then?

I know we talked, Michael and I—we must
have talked, but I don't remember what was said.
Michael had never had that much to say.

Over the years—I know my mind has changed
things—what I imagine as remembering.

Sometimes he whistles and that sweet little dog
comes running from somewhere out in the still darkness;
eyes two black coals afloat in the glow of white
curly hair, a sudden apparition in the porch light.

We'd, all of us, together, named him *Willy*
after *Willy O' Winsbury*—that hero from the song.

#4 Cook Street

You'd stand in the bay window front of the house
and catch the longer views—the Mystic River
off to the north, and the bridge with its slow streaming
of lights at night where one might have expected
to catch a blindered glimpse of sky.
Turn and face south and you saw that strange old house
across Bunker Hill, at the street corner, a three-story
facade of painted clapboard and tall double-hung windows,
broad crown-molded trim, a cornice as it addressed the one street;
weathered shingle and stapled tarpaper presented to the other,
as if that street wasn't a street at all but some dark alley come to light
inadvertently. Two aluminum frame windows randomly placed.
The structure fit with my theories of the post-modern at the time:
the dissolute mustering an obvious, inept pretension, almost poignantly,
like a vagrant in a clean and borrowed shirt and tie, trying his best.
Those days the coal-fueled power plants in Everett had decided
to burn only at night. This was celebrated as improvement by some.
Though the windows were darkened with gritty soot each morning,
you could wash them clean—warm water, ammonia
and old newsprint worked best.
There was no obligation to realize what we breathed at night,
those few of us who slept with the windows opened.

Cinéma vérité

Smoke changes as it moves
from brightness into shadow.
The camera struggles for focus
on dust in the light, movements of a sheer curtain
at an opened window. Street noise is nearly as present
as her voice as we notice she's been speaking, notice
the sound of her voice more than anything said.
Her monologue is oblique, difficult; just as she
is difficult. There's the sense she speaks
of what should already be well understood.
We shoot black and white film, wrong
aperture so's to exaggerate the one dark crease
at the corner of her eye, her luminous skin
vaporous, ghost-like one moment
then stark, all-too-present and flawed as she looks away.
The lens cannot explain itself
There lies the danger in trying to translate
language into film—the woman is left nameless after all,
Conscience, actual memory.

They call film a *time-based media*. I'm not sure that matters
as much as the sound of dry cigarette
meeting flame, the street noise, unintelligible voices,
and the constant, quiet work of gears turning film inside the camera.

Rural free delivery

The moment surfaces, drawn from its clear
chemical bath, this careful dark.

First, there appears the famous mailbox, empty, rusted
metal, shaped as a barn—all its livestock gone;

slowly, ghostly, your image forms then, posed beside the vacant
damaged hull, proud husband of the creatures you'll no longer keep.

The wind must be assumed in this photograph, what it does
this bright day that might explain your strange smile,

what it does to stir the long grass of that unkept field
just outside the camera's view, what it does as your eyes meet lens

and darken a deep well at last empty of what you needed
to drain away, lifting that wounded shoebox sparrow's wing—

the wind, what it brings, what it takes away—that wind
at an empty bottle throat—oh, dear friend, listen how it sings!

Off the boat

As if there were only the one boat,
that's how it struck me
when I first heard the expression.
Maybe my mother and father talked
at the kitchen table
and some one of their acquaintance
was just 'off the boat'
or mom spoke of her own
mother and father when they'd first
come to this country;
Pa working as a day laborer
and her Ma as domestic help.
Pa—Pat Carey was 'just off the boat'
when the molasses vats burst
by the Boston waterfront.
He found pick and shovel work
cleaning up the damage and debris.
His sweetheart, soon-to-be wife, Nora Shea
disembarked in Newport, Rhode Island
—she and her sisters all found work
in the wealthy homes there,
tending to other people's children, household chores.

It was all the one boat though,
as I heard it, that boat they were off.

The stories of that boat too. It sounded a bit like hell
to me, that passage: the dark holds, crowded, lightless,
airless but for the brothy stench of seasick and sweat
all rolling on the dark, green, dangerous sea. [1]
I remember seeing the history book photographs
of men and women and children, crowded cattle

who'd paid their all for the privilege of being herded—
their haunted, harrowed eyes; everything they had,
all their world in bulging sacks carried on their backs.

That one boat: of beautiful hope, desperate escape,
brave passage, ritual humiliation.

Then there was Jeremiah, my great grandfather, dad's side,
the story told so many times I'm sure it's mostly a lie by now
—how he found an out-of-the-way place above deck for the crossing
and slept nights with a coiled rope as his pillow,
watched stars in the salt air.
They were turned away from Boston, waited days outside the harbor.
He finally came to port in Nova Scotia and walked
the thousand miles to a farm in Whitman, Massachusetts
where he had been promised work
—or was it that his dearest darling waited there?

Still it was said of him, after his long, long journey on foot,
when at last he had arrived, that he, too, was just off the boat.

The future that used to be

There was one of those houses involved,
the broad grassy slope risen from river's edge.

to a level place by paned glass doors that never
close right, as if to insist the home's intimacy

with the weather, with chosen friends never shy
of visits unannounced, knowing tea can be made

and conversation had—any hour. And we'd not yet sold
the piano; as such there's no telling who it is we hear

playing that familiar melody. Time marked by embraces;
arrivals, departures fold one into the next, dance-like, slow.

There—*is*—that constant need of house repair—and sorry
sign of my lacking carpentry skill, those telling flaws.

Our children, their complex legacies. We never found
the misplaced keys that would have locked the door.

One Who Climbs Mountains

Windswept bare granite—domed rock peak:
my son, as if seated, struggling, inches himself across
the stone, wide eyed in fear the deafening wind
would take him,
                cast him down.

Years to come we will laugh at the holes worn
in the seat of his pants, my strange joy in watching him,
terror and pride
                and the name he was given that day.

The water tower

You'd climbed with the others to watch
city light move in the dark
like a glowing blood through the veins of some
pulsing organism from a science class film;
noted the mists of breath and smoke rising
even as you lost the thread of their conversation
to the slight wind and your own isolate inattention.

You'd been the first to lie back on cool metal
angled so perfectly for repose,
first to look away from the city　　and up　　at the stars
becoming points of light on a thin black membrane.

You fall with the others as the slight domed top collapses
becoming a sudden shallow dish instead.

The thin steel and its welded perimeter seam holds,
the metal's shock sends a dull thrumming tone
into the water
reverberant dark beneath you.
Hear the water stir and slap as it settles back
into its contained lightless calm.

You hear someone announce an imagined newspaper headline:
"Four Fall, Drown, Foul City Water Supply!"
Another of you moves away then from the pile of bodies
you'd become, beans in the bottom of a bowl.

As he nears its edge the dome rebounds, recovers its shape,
lifts all of you back as suddenly as you'd fallen,
sending again that dull metallic tone into the night,
into the earth, into the city and its—*water supply*
—into your own body,
—into the frightened laughter that, for the moment,
seems　　somehow　　a little better than loneliness.

Chapter 7

The terrible world tells about itself
in the one loud room in an otherwise
quiet house. Television noise.
Something it is wrong to call light
pools and seeps from that tired space
staining this proper darkness close by.

The children watch and learn what they must learn
eventually. Their mother has fallen asleep
I gather and I tarry before her rescue,
step to the sagging porch, sit, crowded to one side
by the japonica so overgrown,
reminded by peeled paint and weathered plank
of my unmet husbandry, tasks, failings;
the yard lunar stone and sand, still
bare from the recent repair of our septic pit

—so costly—so costly. We waited too long.
We'll soon lose this place, I realize
and start at the sudden freedom I feel, admitting this
to myself, sigh at the sad prospect of telling them.

It's late. Tomorrow. I'll explain
this first decision I've made in such a long time.

Always Sunday

Church bells ring. It is that Always Sunday;
back from the bakery up town, the walk
past habit and practice, rite and the race
of Catholics to their large cars.
The century is still beginning, requisite war underway;
home and the house is quiet, its structure low and aching
at its open earth cellar of loose stone and the dark
where the coal was once kept. To the mind of most
neighbors, and despite their kind wishes, we still live
in the murderer's house. They refer to the place
with his name and not ours. They do not know
how the smells of coffee and bacon and toasted bread
rise up to find our children sleeping, adream in the wild nests
we've allowed them. I'll soon call from the foot of that narrow
stair, painted an odd and gorgeous plum color, one cracked
tread mid-flight. I will warn them I am starting the eggs.

The old soldier's cats

They never much liked me.
To be honest, the feeling—or lack
was probably mutual.
The two of them made me feel unwelcome
in the old house. I'd grown up there
yet they'd never admit I belonged.
I'd step through the kitchen door,
John would have offered me coffee—
his horrifying coffee.
One cat might watch from the hall.
The other always hid
as we talked, John and I.
And just as well. By the time I left
my eyes red and burning,
I'd be wheezing to breathe.
Damn cats, I'd say, explaining
the brevity of my visit.

Those times John deployed overseas
it would fall to me to look after those two
and the house, see to their food, shovel their litter,
scrape hair from couch and carpet.
It was the same routine with these
custodial visits; the one would watch
from a safe remove, the other storm off
incensed at the intruding nuisance of the help.
The bolder one would seem to accuse me
about my brother's absence with a fixed stare.
What had I done with the one human
whose company they enjoyed?
As if I'd sent him away
not the politicians in Washington,
our nation's long history of foreign entanglement.

That house had gone to ruin when the old soldier died,
my dear, brave, lonesome brother. The floors were stained and buckled
under the litterbox so in need of changing. The heat wasn't working.

Neither was the plumbing really. The house reeked of poverty and piss.
The stair to the kitchen door was rotted, ready to collapse.
A buyer was found who would take the place as is,
do the necessary repairs to restore its real estate value.
When it came time to remove those cats from the house
the second shyer one was the hardest to gather up.
He hid in the damage under the kitchen sink,
growling, hissing. We'd cornered him there.
It was there he finally surrendered
and, as he did, he let out this sound—
not a howl or crying, it was truly a voice.
God—how it mourned.

Elegy

You'd be pleased to know
I started drinking again
now that you're twenty years gone.

The first few dry years, behind us now,
were all about the dour abstention—
penance and punishment all at once

for the two of us   in the way
it was left for me alone to carry
our argument   never complete

until one day it was forgotten
and sobriety became some kind of rote,
vaguely funereal observance, a token lack

I grew tired of explaining, even to myself.
Just now the late afternoon light
of an October Saturday stumbles in.

It'd gotten dark and the sudden gold
comes as reprieve. I sit and listen
to nothing at all. I sip whisky

and the taste is sweet with blood
from the edge of my tongue
torn ragged on a broken tooth.

The Other Guitar

The weight of this one, the dull sound,
strings dark with dirt and dead,
action on the neck such that every chord
I try seems a high-wire act gone wrong.

Mostly this guitar serves to remind me
of that larger, square-shouldered dreadnaught
I once had—that weighed so much less—its body delicate,
resonant—I played it years with a crack on its face.

That initial damage was my fault. I left it out in the cold
soon after I got it, my thinking the plush lining
of the hardshell case would retain a body warmth
in the way a winter coat with fur lining does.

My lunatic luthier friend laughed when I told him,
then allowed a few lewd comparisons between a guitar
and a woman's body. He worked his repair inside,
hide glue and grafted skin from a salvage mandolin

bridging the break—he did a poor job of it, too, honestly.
That buzzing sound only worse thereafter in certain weather;
particular notes, chords I had to avoid.
Was it then I came to notice the flaw in my own voice?

I don't know if my singing deteriorated.
Maybe my hearing improved.
There was a time there that I blamed the guitar
for what I thought I could sing, what I finally could not.

When I sold it, I thought I'd never have another.

This isn't the first time I've tried

This isn't the first time I've tried
something about that schizophrenic girl
who rode the bus with me out of Syracuse in 1982.

Years back, I sat her down beside a character in a novel,
later felt bad about using her that way.
Once, I tried a poem almost entirely in her voice.

She said she was responsible for all the color in the world.
She'd seen it into being with her eyes.

And, as this was Syracuse, New York, in late November,
early evening, and it had begun to rain, she apologized.
Awfully tired just then. Sorry, sorry

—sorry, she said as the bus pulled away past a chain link fence.
Broken pavement surrounded some fortressed institution.
Square lanterns on metal brackets faced out
their angle seeming a gesture of both greeting and warning.

Monologue or soliloquy—is there a difference?
—or just a crazy person carrying on. Her face was round, pale,
swollen to a softness. Her large dark glasses suggested
glamor—an ironic glamor. This was 1982. The bus mostly dark.

As I remember, she was across the aisle, maybe even a row behind me.
In the seat next to mine a young man with a long beard muttered
prayers to himself constantly, stopped to wash his feet
in a metal bowl every hour or so. His ritual seemed to contain him

completely, absently. I wasn't there, not the girl explaining
her take on the physics and metaphysics of color, her gift, her wearying affliction.
She'd switched on her personal reading light by then, turned it to shine
on her face, smiled up into its bathing flow.

Her face seemed to absorb and resend the light's meek signal
—magnify it somehow. This was tiring work, she explained,
seeing all color into the world—even the purest white—so very tiring.

But what would you do without me?   She went on for our sake,
she went on like that for hours. Did I fall asleep or have I only forgotten
where it was she exited that bus?   I remember after she was gone

there was just the one moment that young, bearded man beside me
met my glance. His eyes widened into mine as if to say something
only to me, though his lips kept moving, uttering his inaudible prayer.

III

Border Music

Dry wind comes through here,
taking with it dust and seed.
Nothing is promised.

The desert floor marks
what's fallen, tells the story
where sky's mere witness

fails.
    Days of blind light,
blessed light, blistering light,
then shattering stars—

Night,
      I last held him
then, saying his name, his name
      that I pray he keeps.

Shelter Cove

I am awake and the crowded harbor quiet
as even the practice of leisure involves respite.
Pleasure boats barely stir at their moorings,
their motion subtle as the breath of calm sleep.

What water one can see from this sheltered porch
three stories up presents a dark green mirror, opaque,
vacant seeming, still a dreamless blank as first light
changes the sky opposite. Distant jet aircraft contrail

as pencil line contrasts with the soft brushwork cirrus
clouds colored like corn silk, bruised flesh, diluted wine;
all of this on that broad palest blue, nearly white canvas.
Three shore birds of a species I cannot name light upon

the mansard edge not forty feet from where I watch and write,
their cries mock the day arriving. No one should call it song.

That summer of monuments

Washington, DC, 2017

That day The Grant Memorial was being restored,
parts of it closed to public access, covered in tarps,
it felt like trespass stepping onto the marble terrace
and approaching the monument figures—
soldiers on horseback,
their banner unfolding, swords drawn.
The men's faces mostly blank, the horses
more plainly urgent with panic, terror.
One horse has fallen, his rider is thrown,
the man's face there at an eye level
just above the trampled bronze earth,
so hot to the touch in the August sunlight.

In the buzzing summer silence it seems
you can hear the hoove-thunder,
the creaking wheels of artillery caissons,
screams of man and animal.

Above all the wild motion in darkened bronze,
positioned on the memorial architecture's high pedestal,
General Grant and his horse are at rest,
their attention set upon some distant action
in this squinting midday summer haze.

Always July

I

Always, its wisps of wood smoke,
ocean noise, salt breeze, surf rhythm

a pressure in the shore sand at our feet
comments on the immediate

and precious as our children run past,
their shouts blurred, then erased in the chaotic

churn of it all. Our closer, quieter conversations
sorting trouble. And long walks with nothing

said, as the wind will not allow it, and it's good.
Stone jetties to mark, reaching at water.

II

I write this early an April or November morning
and note there was some rain last night; the sky

remains a pale scrim drawn somewhere between
here and the sunlight; here where the air is so still,

still except for the remote occasional stir of the car
that passes in the street unseen. Look out my window

and three backyards away the two plastic pinwheels
revolve absently on a child's play structure, spun there

by that infrequent wake of passing car, the soft whisper
of travel on the wet street toward the sweet elsewhere.

Stone Mountain, Georgia

Waiting on the summer night
not yet dark enough, we can watch
as dozens of young kids dash and weave
about happily through the settling crowd,
brandishing sword-like wands.

These glow different colors on signal
—watermelon red, police-light blue,
a pale—almost-white—neon green.

They light at random now. It will be quite the spectacle
once the laser light show begins
and all the hundreds of swords turn together
one color   then the next.
A shrill hawker announces over the public address
that there's still time to purchase
one of these toys
at the park's conveniently located concessions.

Loud music resumes playing then
—the bass line a preconscious throb.
We've settled ourselves into lawn chairs,
balanced them against the hillside incline.

The slope forms a natural theater
facing the mountainside,
three equestrian figures carved there in bas-relief.
Two sisters and their children appear
—the space just in front of us.
I only guess the women are sisters—it's the children,
an easy familiarity only cousins ever have.

Their dark skin, small statures, hair jet black,
the shape of their features: they could be Aztecs or Mayans
travelled here through time
for some adoration of the mountainside.
They spread blankets and lay out baskets of food.

The young ones vibrate as much as they dance
to the music, all the thrilling crowd.
They form a line at the lead edge of their blanket,
facing the mountain like us, and begin
clumsily blocking the pop-song choreography they know.

From somewhere close behind me
an old woman I assume is the grandmother
arrives with the smallest, youngest of the cousins
holding her hand.
The old woman sits, settles the child into her lap, has her sip
from a straw in a plastic cup.

The child's black, black eyes, unblinking—brimming
with her cousins, the crowd, the mountain, the dance, the dimming sky
—her eyes seem to enlarge, to deepen, darken.

The music stops, changes.
It's night enough finally and the lights are about to begin.

Tomorrow it will rain—late afternoon, one of those rains like you get
down here in Georgia that come down, down, down.

It is that season of the year with rain like that each day; clockwork,
torrential, scouring, and washing every last thing.

Quaking Aspen

Smoke rises from our fire
seeming to insist
on the night sky available
at the open hole
in the leafy canopy
above our camp,
long aspens
attendant—
firelight gold splashing
slender limbs.
The bald promontory
across the access road
the sky there like soothing
ambient noise,
       the milk white stone
broken through
treeline and earth,
fractured itself,
loose fitted rock
I don't trust
climbing at night.

My daughter, her lover, their dog
leave for the wider display
of stars, wandering satellites,
the mountain glowing
at their feet.
I am just as happy here
by the fire,
this odd column of smoke
drawn now in my
direction
slightly
such that it stings my eyes.

D&C

Outside the clinic two women stood some distance
from the door and held signs and watched silently
as we entered. One held out the image of a fetus;
the other Jesus Christ.
      Denise held fast to my arm.

I don't recall how long we waited
in that room much larger than it needed to be,
all the empty chairs. I remember Denise so quiet
and that young woman, a girl really. She stood there
looking impatient, inconvenienced, as her parents
sat close by—I assumed them the parents.
The girl stood as if to sit was surrender somehow.
She would only wait so long—
The woman I'd decided was the girl's mother
looked up at her without expression, black, blank,
unblinking so as to hold her child in place
and the father beside her sat, seethed, stared
so fixedly at his hands.

I remember all the arguments
as we sat, silent:
Denise and I,
that family, if it was a family
      —how everyone was wrong.

At General Sherman's keep

We wait by the gated park entrance
minding our daughter's anxious dog,
the small, sweet mongrel rescue
just now thinking his girls might never come back.

My wife and I have had our turn visiting the sequoia;
our daughter and her lover now take theirs—
the dog's not allowed in near the monument trees.

My wife is pleased with the small watercolor travel kit.
The case unfolds neatly on her lap, the hinged pigment tray cover
becomes a well for water on one side, a place for brushes on the other.

She paints small, imperfect circles in a gold sepia
onto pocket-sized squares of paper, she paints
and listens to *what*-I-don't-know on her earbuds.

She's absented herself in this way, even as we sit
close together, done this as much for my sake, I think,
knowing I've pledged at least three journal pages each day.

I've this moment to write and she has gone that place
she goes when working, thinking or decidedly not

thinking, the shapes at her brush tip repeating
and joining to find some pattern, a texture,

some otherwise un-nameable diagrammatic fact
with that scary courage of hers where honesty

precedes understanding.
                    She trusts what she does not know.

Our daughter and her lover are due back
—*soon*, I console the dog,
dog-years factored, the same age as me.

If you see the Buddha

Ginsburg wrote of encountering
Walt Whitman in the supermarket
more than fifty years ago.
Maybe it was Robert Lowell who reminded me.
I've seen him a number of times lately,
first noticed him as he researched something
on the public computer terminal
at the local library; since then I've spotted him
out and about town.
He rides around on a tricycle.
No matter the weather.
The poet wears a dark blue visored captain's hat,
an antique; small brass letters across the front indicate
he had some position of responsibility aboard the Titanic.
I don't recall any mention of this in the poet's biography.
I've thought and thought better
of approaching him to inquire on the subject.

I was asked about the Buddha though.

Not certain, but I do believe I've seen Him
twice actually, or I should say in two different incarnations.
There is a frail old man who sits in front of me at mass on Sunday;
stooped, skeletal, weary, His body slow moving, achingly.
He turns to me and takes my hand
at the prescribed moment in the mass
each and every week
and He wishes me peace.

My other encounter was with a much fatter and younger manifestation.
This past December, like Ginsburg with Whitman, it was in a supermarket.
A toddler riding the grocery cart fold-down seat.
His legs jutted unbending through the two provided
holes. His older brother rode in the body of the carriage.
Their father had parked them aside so he could pick
through the bagels stocked into plastic bins
for the early Sunday morning shoppers.

I waited my turn behind the father and I glanced
at the boy and our eyes met.
I watched then
as He searched my face
and across His own there passed this look of recognition.

We said nothing to each other.
Neither of us possessed the vocabulary.
There were no words.
There are no words.
He nodded,
          we smiled.

Like a glove

I'd have thought my brother would be disappointed
getting a baseball glove for Christmas,

about as useful in the middle of a New England winter
as a snorkel and pair of swim fins.

But that glove was exactly what he'd wished for;
the autograph of his favorite player branded
onto the leather thumb.

That winter-into-spring the glove and he would become one
in a kind of ritual process, a baptismal rite and more.
He soaked the thing in brine, then bound it with twine;
a softball clasped within.

It seemed every other day he was oiling its surfaces
or working them with saddle soap.

Nights he slept with the thing bedded
between his mattress and box spring.

He'd face the ceiling in the dark of our room,
dreaming but not sleeping, odd combination
of the princess and the pea and the penitent
on a bed of nails.

My brother's approach to baseball
involved a stoic pride, born of humility,
courage in the face of suffering.

You see, he wasn't a gifted ballplayer,
wasn't so much an athlete as an acetic.

I remember his favorite player at the time
led the league in getting hit by the pitch.
HBP wasn't a statistic most fans paid attention to.
      For Dan it resonated.

He took that same approach at the plate when he batted,
crowding in close, holding his ground, taking one for the team.
His eyesight was such that he never hit very well,
but he had that way of getting on base.

Yet in the field—he played right field—
the ball hit his way always had a way
of finding his glove—
magic, magnetic,
the way water's found by a divining stick.

It came to me years later, that glove.
My brother had concluded an undistinguished career
by most measures.

Still, there was majesty in the moment
he handed it down.
In that moment and thereafter,
the supple skin,
the history of devotion—
his hand touched mine whenever I wore it.

Keepsake shirt

I set aside the one white shirt for myself,
chose to reclaim its whiteness, as everything in that house
had eventually taken on a patina of nicotine or a coating
of dust and cat hair, or simply somehow grayed with age.

Hot water and bleach did the trick though
and I liked the notion of keeping that shirt.
It was a heavy fabric, well made, shirttails long enough
there was a chance I could keep them tucked.

And I liked the idea of keeping him that way, his old shirt.
I wore the thing most of that first summer.
Then, as happens from time to time, laundry day
I reached into the dryer to find one of my ball point pens

had secreted its way into the wash unnoticed.
This time there was more than the ordinary anger,
at more than just myself, at God or fate, or whatever force
in the universe has so ruled, that I cannot keep anything.

Pharoah's Horsemen

Twenty years later, I'm not sure she's ever forgiven
her mother for singing in that Handel oratorio
where at one point the chorus recounts how Pharoah's army
was lost, Moses having closed the path behind him
in the parted waters of the Red Sea
—all that excited singing about the cavalry and their horses drowned.

I still remember the way my neighbor's daughter looked over at me,
tears in her eyes, the ancient tragedy so real for her just then.
"The horses never did anyone harm," she said, she seethed
at Stupid God.   I tried my best to signal sympathy
with a smile. I knew her only well enough to know
at the time that horses meant a great deal to her.

Still, we're not so close I can claim to know her.
Honestly, things I've heard over the years scare me,
that dangerous anger, so difficult to explain,
the constant smolder, the sudden flames.

I wonder would it have done her good that day to tell her
something of my own fondness, not for horses,
but for the soldiers in Pharoah's army,
the ones who made it home but always carried with them
a sodden after-weight of their experience,

the burden of a shortened temper,
a cough, a shallowness of breath
            that one soldier I loved
                always blamed it on cigarettes.

The Whistlepig

A dog has chased him here
through the different yards that face
our dead-end street. The dog—frantic, territorial,

knows, though, to stop at the loose gravel
marking the end of our drive.

A tapered wall of mortarless stone dies there
to nothing that side of the house no one goes.

That old shed a study
in dilapidation, the compost we've never learned
to tend correctly.   Our friend takes his rest there,

leans back on his haunches, sunlight
warming his gut, his jaw works side to side on fare
he's stolen from other gardens.

The door to that shed will not shut.

Neighbors haven't yet voiced their displeasure
at his survival, his sanctuary there—here with us.

I know they soon will. And that we'll lose this place, too.
Just now, though, I hear that song playing

"The Diggers" with that line about—*the sin of property*
that—*we do disdain*—anthem that it is.

Then and there

As the poets ran long, I'd resigned
to not reading at all. Time was short.
Others needed the studio at a fixed time.

It's in this confusion, perhaps, some aspect of my defense
left mistakenly and waited outside
in the parking lot, leaned against the car
smoking hand rolled cigarettes
—some such ghost, gone.
                        And as I did have my turn
at the microphone, camera light blinding me,
this other
spirit arrived to catch the words
in my throat.

I heard my own voice
sound that last warped note
you hear from a broken guitar string.

I did not weep.
I promise you that much, my brother,
but you were in that room.
And something so suddenly, achingly,
finally was said
then and there

though, I doubt I managed
an intelligible word.

IV

Notes on demolition

for Denise

The grinning advice got from a mason
friend of mine I told of our plans
was that in demolishing a chimney
one should start at the top
and work their way down.
Seriously though, with firm hammer strikes at the masonry
the old mortar will crumble, fall away.
Pry the brick loose,
one, then the next, then the next.
He'd shown me the proper use of brick tongs
as well, how to carry enough each load
for the tool to serve its purpose.
The weight, the work strangely pleasing
the first few trips down narrow stairs
two floors to the basement
where I staged out debris.
~
Then I notice one brick fall into the shaft
I've opened—and I'm the clever one to realize
it one less brick for me to carry
and soon I'm thrilled at the easy way
whole courses hammer loose
and drop into the deep stir
of dust and dark—such an elegant process,
as if the chimney's 'stack effect' reversed
itself after a hundred years
smoke rendering back unto flame.
The brick will be waiting in the cellar
to be sorted and stacked for hauling away—
this I tell myself, so pleased with the ingenuity.
~
Bounding down the stair to inspect,
I stop, stare
        dumbstruck.
~

We'd set up camp in the first floor living room
as nomadic urban pioneers;
our bed and a television set, a microwave oven,
the crib, though most nights our son slept between us.
We'd lived like this a while, always the one
        room habitable
while we tore apart the next.

Now, I am stunned and stopped,
my gaze fixed upon the scene
of our ragged domesticity
rendered in sudden, seamless
black, an eerie dis-reflection of light,
dust fine as powder, black as coal,
        blacker.
I'd thought the brick would fall clear.
First one caught, then more.
The shaft, then the plaster
broke—breached—
        billowed black over it all.

    All.

Beautiful. I tell you   beautiful
black snowscape   capture of light,
light claimed, subsumed
into an anthracitic jewel surfacing
of every form: the blinded clock—black,
        a chair—black,
the trunk we use as a table, the crib
        —black—black.
I know that I must clean this all
before you return, the refugee with our son
and all our worries in tow,
all that you carry,
even our daughter not yet born.
And I know I must leave no telling traces
and that I'll only tell you
carefully later
what I see now,

years later, still,
that this secretly—for me—
deepened every color since.

The box spring

The soft old mattress complied as passage
through the narrow stair hall required—
dull weight, an old friend too tired to resist.
The box spring proved the greater challenge.

At the old house we'd only managed, removing
the tall double-hung window sashes and fitting
the rigid form to the diagonal of the opening.
Here, finally, we sawed through the wooden flat,

bent the spring of it back like the trigger on a gun,
tied it fast and gently fitted the tense, folded shape
through the hall, the stair, the door into the room;
finally eased it onto the slatted bed frame and cut

the binding ropes, stood back from the sudden
crash arrival in that room, a sense of the past's ill fit
and no idea between us if we'd ever move again.

The recording session

for Walker

He bows forward, head turned to one side, listening
to the already recorded parts in headphones.
Now I watch his hands move the button accordion,
his hands, together then apart, pushing then pulling
evenly, so slowly the low droned note,
hear that slight scrape, something loose in the thing
—something he said he'd meant to have fixed by now.
Sonic accident, the engineer worries, will ruin the take:
a car horn outside, someone coughing, a door closes nearby.
And yet all are agreed the window open in the attic studio
is worth the risk of flaw this warm summer afternoon.
See the plastic blind, just touching the window jamb,
moved as if a reluctant answer
                                to the whispering leaves,
the delicate tree branch gesture at the blue sky there.
What seems like breath enters the otherwise airless room.
Melody—new melody—this his easy invention. I listen
as my own unknown song, with its several mistaken words,
is reimagined and becomes, just this moment, so clear.

Cynthia's time

This same city was different then.
At any point you might be taken
with the light reflected off
new buildings or the river
as it flowed near then underneath
some one of the arched bridge spans
and you could imagine her enjoying the same
light, her generous attention,
just as the stranger met out walking alone
could be someone as blessed
in her acquaintance
as we were then,
in her gracious calm,
her constant way of proving loneliness false.

O—I know it rained in those years, it would've
had to; but I don't believe it ever fell so cold.

Always love

And which of you comes to meet me
at the table by a window, that room of fragrance
and melancholy I imagined so clearly—

I would want the old friend who was always a comfort to me.
But then I remember how that version of you would complain,
albeit with a smile, of old bones, past beauty, sweetest days

long gone. Surely, you'd prefer to be that grinning girl instead, shy
and laughing to realize her silly vanity in a cousin's photograph.

Or maybe you are the small child who does not yet know
her brother's suffering. She holds his hand,
obedient and adoring his handsome, undamaged face.

Or would you arrive in the company
of your first son, and he, the shining soldier
never gone to his war?

I know you would want to be your father's daughter
where you might finally have the breath to dance to his music.

And what about my songs,
would they finally catch your ear,
turn your terrible, delicate heart?

Would you be the woman who took my father's hand and led him
toward the house that day it was raining, falling so very hard
upon the dry, bare earth?

Guitars

Pale light of a summer
no longer night not yet morning—
it seems the music's conversation will not end.
We've taken it out into the street after closing time.
It does not matter exactly whose song it is.
Our voices combine in an intricate harmony.
Hewitt, he calls himself 'The Poet Savior of Rock and Roll'
—and only half-jokingly, I think he's the genius
of this particular arrangement.
Oen changes chord position on guitar, his face leaning
forward as he sings as if to immerse himself in sound.
And Nick plays one of those fills he used to play
—seeming so effortless,
wild and quiet at once, his form of prayer.

Memorial familiar

New grass grown in thick, starting
to occlude the two VA-supplied
memorial plaques set into the ground:
small frames, leathery-brown,
braid-bordered, each showing name,
military rank, the war fought;
for each the simple cross to mark a Christian,
brighter, brassy and pronounced against the darker
background surface.

I pull at the grass where it's closed in
and won't tear easily. I try
—and find it clotted, flesh-like,
gripped like sod-welt surrounding wounds.

Reaching under, my fingers work
edges that finally give
and sharp black ants come spilling out
across the warm bronze,
climb my hands and forearms, biting.

Frantic, quiet hurrying, I carry the tufts torn loose
across the access road to some overgrown brush
untended piles of other refuse
thrown there tell me I'm free
to do the same: soiled, stinging work
that this is, remembering them.

The way it is

I've long ago forgotten anything I meant to say
or anything I wanted him to say, that last time
I saw my father. I've forgiven him the trivial talk
of the better road to take from his place to hospital
and leaving it unspoken, whatever it was I needed
said that was not said about the simple fact of his going.
It took me some years to process, but this quiet
has come, or call it peace, forgiveness, grace, at long last,
the sweeter, kinder memories allowed. I haven't the logic
or language to describe it or even give it proper thanks.
I've only noticed it recently, as just the way it is.

Empathy

Toward the end he could barely speak;
then you'd never much cared for his talk,
harsh jokes always gone too far, come too soon
     after calamity.

Come his own death, though, the snide remarks
could be forgiven. His past laughter at others' expense
seemed somehow his right by retroactive bargain.

and with your visit he managed the one last joke,
intended anyone who might ask him
     too much otherwise:
Not sure when I'll be back to work—then a smile.

And did your kindness come in accepting this.
the sad lie or the dry wit, whatever it was not said?

Citizen Cain

There is something to be said
for having one's worst fears realized,
wisdom that comes of scarred survival.

The spare slice of bread
comes a glory to those starved for it;
rain so welcome in a season of drought.

The politician never spoke so stirringly
—with such candor and grace—
as when finally conceding the election.

We speak so kindly of the dead.

Perhaps you are a fervent patriot
who must watch as your country
commits atrocity.

You needn't love it any less, that country
that failed your brother's pain,
his laughter, the strange music of his suffering.
The weight of this.

Once you've been broken there is a different tenderness.

The Widow's House

I'd not yet let my hair grow long
—was still glad of your smooth chin,

that devil's grin when talk was allowed
on matters just a tad less serious.

Oh, summer nights, there on the road
to Parknasila, that place called Drimna More.

Brier tangled at a clearing by the stream,
in the thrall of our own illicit music

—wanting nothing as it seemed
I'd all the luck and love of both the boys—

my sweet scholar with his tongue still whole,
the shy, sly soldier stolen secretly away.

Weren't our notions large   those few weeks
before conspiracy met with consequence?

Oh, sweet smell of bread in the kitchen
masking the stench of sweat and shite

and blood. How the cormorant will dive
where a heron circles, circles wide.

October now, smoke of other fires wafts in.
There rises the same damnable moon

as in that terrible season. Dogs bark
faintly, only out of habit.

Parge fails, clag falls from stone.
If you mean to visit send one of your children

on ahead to warn me.   I'll warm the place.
I seldom bother on my own.

The Champion of Doubt

My father would announce to me,
every now and then, in conversation,
"I've forgotten more than you'll ever know!"
—always a wry grin, pleased
with himself, with the elegant formulation:
that subtle trace of self-deprecation,
along with the more pronounced teasing slight for his son.
"They could fill books—books
—with all the things you don't know."
That was the other turn of phrase
—often followed upon the first.
This sounds maybe crueler than it was ever intended
though my ignorance was indeed his meaning.
Sometimes to soften the effect he'd have put on one
of his comedic accents—he had a number of them:
the French sophisticate, the precise German, a jolly Brit
with a Cockney delivery, and another Englishman
of most exquisitely refined diction.
One of his favorites was a Jew, the voice vaguely rabbinical,
appropriated from the standup of Myron Cohen, Mel Brooks.
Just the beginning of some tension between us would need diffusing
He'd turn, as if to someone invisible in the room, and offer in that voice,
"I taught him everything I know and still he knows nothing."
You might read the comment as insult; but you would be mistaken,
I know—I was there, I heard it said and I know
how it was so much more importantly his confession,
more resignation than prayer—but no less his blessing.

Joy

for Ilya and Adam

In this joke, this particular joke that isn't a joke at all really,
it's two poets crossing the street where one says to the other
as if they'd been having the conversation all along,
I don't believe in happiness, only joy.

Music was like this for me, singing
a song was a terrifying thought until it didn't matter
anymore, the singing, and there was only the song.

This was a realization that only lasted a while. To be honest,
it wasn't quite—realized—and was quickly forgot.

It's just there are more important words than prayers
hidden in your mouth like flecks of gold in riverwash sand
to catch the light of certain moments, so precious.

And deeper still there's the diamond silence—

It's when you realize you'll never grasp it
that the prisoner is set free.

Set the prisoner free.

That River

Hands cup the clear water
and shape a lens of pale light
for the old man to witness
each crease in skin and callous
clarified   magnified
one forgotten scar noted though
the wound that brought it about
is beyond recollection
he observes the prayer-like
gesture of lifting water
to the mouth to drink
    drink slowly
he reaches again watching
for his own reflection
and sees instead that river

Acknowledgements

Grateful acknowledgment to the publications where some of these poems first appeared:

'Off the boat' appears in 'Yearning to Breathe Free' by Moonstone Arts Center

'To History' appears in Footnote #8 by Alternating Current Press

'This isn't the first time' was awarded Third Place for The Frank O'Hara Prize by the Worcester County Poetry Association and together with 'The Widow's House' appears in The Worcester Review.

'Notes on Demolition' was selected as an Editor's Choice for The Allen Ginsberg Prize by The Passaic County Community College Poetry Association and appears in Paterson Literary Review.

'Border Music' appears in What Rough Beast by Indolent Books.

Special thanks to poet, Alan Feldman—the examples you offer through your work, through your generous teaching, through your thoughtful criticism—these are truly cherished gifts.

In further thanks I start rattling off names: Polly Brown, Oen Kennedy, Hewitt Huntwork, John Boehmer, Nick Post, Jan Hutchinson, Joel Moscowitz, Miriam Levine, Charles Coe, Walker Anderson, Susan Levine, Gary Snyder, Joe Baskowski, Rose Polenzani, Jef Scoville. I'm left feeling indebted to each of you in your own way and in the best possible way—forever.

And, of course, Denise, Jeremiah, Hannah.

Tom Driscoll's poetry has appeared in *Scapegoat Review, The Worcester Review, Paterson Literary Review, Oddball Magazine, Carcosa Magazine, Decadent Review, Drawn To The Light, What Rough Beast* by Indolent Books and Moonstone Arts Center's *Poetry Ink* and *Yearning to Breathe Free* Anthologies.

Tom's poem 'Duty Leave Home' won the Robert P. Collén Poetry Prize in 2017. 'Notes on Demolition' was selected an Editor's Choice for the Allen Ginsberg Prize and 'This isn't the first time' received Third Place in The Frank O'Hara Prize—both in 2021.

www.ingramcontent.com/pod-product-compliance
Lightning Source LLC
Chambersburg PA
CBHW031124160426
43192CB00008B/1106